LUGE

BY ASHLEY GISH

CREATIVE EDUCATION
CREATIVE PAPERBACKS

Published by Creative Education and Creative Paperbacks
P.O. Box 227, Mankato, Minnesota 56002
Creative Education and Creative Paperbacks are imprints of
The Creative Company
www.thecreativecompany.us

Design by The Design Lab
Production by Rachel Klimpel
Art direction by Rita Marshall

Photographs by Alamy (dpa picture alliance, Tribune Content
Agency LLC), AP Images (ASSOCIATED PRESS, Michael Kap-peler/
picture-alliance/dpa, Anke Waelischmiller/SVEN SIMON/picture-
alliance/dpa), Dreamstime (Lukas Blazek), Getty Images
(The Denver Post), iStockphoto (Aksonov), Newscom (ZUMA Press),
Shutterstock (trekandshoot)

Library of Congress Cataloging-in-Publication Data
Names: Gish, Ashley, author.
Title: Luge / Ashley Gish.
Series: Amazing Winter Olympics.
Includes bibliographical references and index.
Summary: Celebrate the Winter Games with this high-interest intro-
duction to luge, the sport known for its sleds and icy courses. Also
included is a biographical story about slider Shiva Keshavan.

Identifiers:
ISBN 978-1-64026-497-7 (hardcover)
ISBN 978-1-68277-049-8 (pbk)
ISBN 978-1-64000-627-0 (eBook)
This title has been submitted for CIP processing under LCCN
2021938164.

Table of Contents

The first luge competition took place in 1883. The racecourse was a 2.5-mile (4 km) road in Davos, Switzerland. In 1964, luge was included in the Winter Olympic Games at Innsbruck, Austria. Germany dominated the sport early on.

Countries like Germany have snowy mountains with good areas for building outdoor courses.

Sleds and sliders are weighed before the race, and lighter athletes are allowed to add weights to their bodies.

Athletes steer sleds down a curvy, ice-covered course. **Sliders** lie face-up on the sled. Their legs stick straight out in front of them. They point their toes to go faster. Sliders reach speeds of up to 90 miles (145 km) per hour.

sliders another term for luge athletes

The Winter Olympics have four luge events. These are men's singles, women's singles, doubles, and team relay. One slider rides during singles luge. In doubles, two athletes ride a slightly heavier sled.

In doubles luge, the larger person is usually on top and does most of the steering.

For team relays, three sleds from each nation complete the course, one after the other. The team with the fastest time wins the relay race.

Sensors are used to time races to within a thousandth of a second.

Special race boots help sliders keep their legs and feet straight.

Sliders wear **aerodynamic** bodysuits. They also wear helmets. Spiked gloves give sliders **traction** as they pull themselves along the ice at the start of the race.

aerodynamic having a shape that allows air to move past without pushing the object back

traction the grip of an object on a surface

Athletes use a pair of handles to rock themselves back and forth before pushing off.

Sleds are short and narrow. The first sleds were made from wood. Today, they are made of **fiberglass**. The underside of the sled has steel runners. Sleds weigh 50 to 59 pounds (22.6–26.8 kg). They do not have brakes.

fiberglass a strong material made from a mix of glass and plastic fibers

Races are based on speed. Sliders go down the racecourse a few times. They control the sled by slightly shifting their weight. Then the slider's times are added up. The racer with the fastest total time wins the event.

An Olympic track is usually made of concrete covered by about two inches (5.1 cm) of ice.

In 2014, Erin Hamlin became the first American woman to win an Olympic luge medal. She took the bronze in luge singles in Sochi, Russia.

Erin Hamlin competed in luge events in 2006, 2010, 2014, and 2018.

Fearless sliders fly down icy tracks. They race to the finish as fast as they can. Watch this heart-stopping sport during the next Winter Olympics.

A luge course is usually less than 1 mile (1.6 km) long and drops about 400 feet (122 m) in that span.

Competitor Spotlight: Shiva Keshavan

Shiva Keshavan is from the Himalayan region of India. He started out by sledding on paved mountain roads. He began training for luge in Austria at age 15. In 1998, Keshavan was the first and only Indian luge competitor at the Winter Olympics. He was also the youngest luge Olympian in history. He competed in six Winter Games. Now he is a luge trainer.

Read More

Johnson, Robin. *Bobsleigh, Luge, and Skeleton*. New York: Crabtree, 2010.

Loh-Hagan, Virginia. *Extreme Street Luging*. Ann Arbor, Mich.: Cherry Lake, 2016.

Waxman, Laura Hamilton. *Bobsled and Luge*. North Mankato, Minn.: Amicus, 2017.

Websites

Kiddle: Luge Facts for Kids
https://kids.kiddle.co/Luge
Find out about luge history, rules, and gear at this site.

Sports Illustrated Kids: The View from the Sled During an Olympic Luge Run
https://www.sikids.com/olympics/view-sled-during-olympic-luge-run
See firsthand what it is like to ride a luge!

Note: Every effort has been made to ensure that the websites listed above are suitable for children, that they have educational value, and that they contain no inappropriate material. However, because of the nature of the Internet, it is impossible to guarantee that these sites will remain active indefinitely or that their contents will not be altered.

Index